Produced for Gallery Books by Joshua Morris Publishing, Inc.
167 Old Post Road, Southport, Connecticut 06490

Best Behavior™ is a trademark owned by
Joshua Morris Publishing, Inc.
All rights reserved.

ISBN 0-8317-0755-0

Printed in Hong Kong.

A Child's Guide to
Manners at School

• RULES •

1. OBEY THE CROSSING GUARD

2. DON'T RUN IN THE HALLS

3. ALWAYS BE ON TIME

4. NO TALKING IN LINE

You probably think that school has enough rules. Here are a few more. *These* rules can make the difference between a good day or a bad day at school.

Rise and Shine!

Make sure you have your homework, notebook, lunch, money, yoyo, and anything you need. That way you won't make yourself late or hold up your ride by running back home for things you forgot.

Be kind to your bus driver. Some drivers love to hear all 29 verses of "I found a Peanut." Others find any kind of noise distracting. Follow the driver's rules. It's more polite — and safer!

It's okay to be late now and then, but not every day. If you're late, ask your parents to write a note explaining your tardiness to your teacher. Apologize to everyone: the principal, the teacher, the carpool driver and the other riders.

When you get to school, you may meet some friendly people—and some not-so-friendly...

Friendly kids. Be friendly to them and you'll be everyone's hero. Be mean to them, and they may get *you* in trouble.

Unfriendly kids. It's best to avoid people who try to tease you. If you can't talk an unfriendly kid out of giving you a hard time, find an older friendly kid who will stand up for you. And if you think you're in danger, tell a teacher.

The Principal. It's the principal's job to make sure everyone is safe, and that things run smoothly. Be polite. Don't say or write anything rude or unkind about a person that might get back to him or her.

The Substitute Teacher. Lots of people pick on subs. Imagine teaching a class full of people you don't know, with a schedule you don't know, in a classroom you don't know. It's bound to be a long, hard day for a sub. Don't make it worse. Try to be fair, friendly, and helpful.

The Teacher. You are an important person to your teacher. He or she may even dream of you at night. Do you want those to be dreams — or nightmares?

Your Friends.

You will see most of these people every day, all year, and maybe for years to come. Try not to put having a good time with your friends before doing your best in school.

You don't have to be best friends with everyone. But it's smart to be on good terms with most people. Unless you want enemies...

...don't steal

...don't lie

...don't cheat

...and don't tell on people — unless someone is in danger, or someone is stealing, lying, or cheating.

You may have some sticky problems at school . . . You don't feel well. Your stomach hurts. Your old soccer injury is acting up. Or you're exhausted from staying up late to watch "Godzilla Eats Cleveland."

Even if it's a bad day, try to pay attention. If you really feel awful, tell your teacher.

A friend wants you to do something wrong.

Think about it.
It may be against the rules.
You may feel bad about it.

You may be afraid of getting
into trouble.

You just might not want to do it.

In the classroom . . .

Respect everyone's privacy.

That includes the teacher.

Don't make fun of—or make faces at—someone who gives a
speech or report. The same rule goes if someone gives a wrong
answer or needs extra help. Don't make fun of anybody!

Keep a neat desk. Don't leave food or anything else that doesn't belong at school in your desk.

Always hang up your hat and coat where they belong. If you're messy in the coatroom or with your locker—you could lose something valuable one day!

Be quiet about your report card—it's rude to brag or snoop.

On the playground...

Let someone join your team, even if he or she isn't very good at the game you're playing.

Take turns. Don't use your size to push people around.

If you borrow equipment, remember to take it back.

In the cafeteria . . .

Wait your turn in the cafeteria line. Don't grab.

Be nice to the people behind the counters.

Use good table manners.

When you go, don't leave a mess behind.

In general . . .

You don't have your homework.

Your teacher will probably understand if you miss your homework once or twice. But don't make a habit of it.

If you tell stories to get out of every situation, your teacher will not trust you.

If you miss the bus home, borrow the office phone to call your parents or a neighbor. If you can't reach anyone at home and you have your keys, ask the principal or a teacher for a ride home.

SCHOOL'S OUT! You may feel like bursting out the door and racing away. What should you really do?